Turning
Problem
Employees
Into
SUCCESSES

A Handbook for Managers and Supervisors

Carol Cox Smith

JOHNSON INSTITUTE®

Minneapolis

Copyright © 1992 Carol Cox Smith

Johnson Institute
7205 Ohms Lane
Minneapolis, MN 55439-2159
(612) 831-1630

Library of Congress Cataloging-in-Publication Data

Smith. Carol Cox.
    Turning problem employees into successes: a handbook for managers and supervisors / Carol Cox Smith.
       p. c.m.
    Includes bibliographical references.
    ISBN 1-56246-029-3
    1. Problem employees. 2. Employee assistance programs. 3. Supervision of employees—Handbooks, manuals, etc. I. Title.
HF5549.5.E42S58 1991
658.3'045—dc20

91-32662
CIP

Printed in the United States of America

1 2 3 4 5 6 / 97 96 95 94 93 92

Contents

Acknowledgments

I wish to express special thanks to Joyce Wilson, Ph.D., Lynessa Gallagher, Florence Parnegg, and Steve Anderson for their valuable editorial help.

Goals of This Book

T *urning Problem Employees Into Successes* takes a unique look at a serious question facing managers and supervisors:

What should we do about "problem employees?"

"Problem employees" are those persons whose job performance is below standard because of their use of alcohol or other drugs; or whose problems with family, finances, or general mental health (such as depression or stress) lower their productivity and spoil their relationships with other employees.

The answer to the above question is:

Problem employees need to be identified, confronted, and referred in order to improve their work performance.

Since managers and supervisors are the ones most likely to work with problem employees on a daily basis, they are the best persons to do *identification, confrontation,* and *referral.* However, managers and supervisors need training to handle these responsibilities effectively.

This book will train managers and supervisors in the referral process. "Referral" may be defined as "using company and community resources to assess problems and recommend solutions that will improve employee performance." The process consists of five steps:

1. Documenting work performance problems.
2. Identifying problem employees based on work performance standards.
3. Eliminating enabling, the principal barrier to referral.
4. Knowing company and community resources.
5. Taking action to confront problem employees successfully.

This book provides case examples taken from real companies and exercises that show managers and supervisors how to apply the five steps of referral to their own department.

Turning Problem Employees Into Successes can be used effectively in the following ways:

Individual self-study. This handbook is self-instructional. Managers and supervisors can read it and work the exercises at their own pace. Many adults learn best in a self-directed way, without teachers, classrooms, or tests.

Group discussions and workshops. EAPs can assign sections of this book for individual reading, then use the reading to stimulate problem-solving discussion in small-group settings. Or EAPs can use this handbook as the primary teaching tool for workshops and seminars.

Off-site training. This handbook can be sent to managers and supervisors who are unable to attend on-site training sessions. It can also be a helpful tool for video classes and conferences.

Professional development. Administrators or EAPs can offer professional development credits for completing this handbook.

Quick reference. Managers and supervisors can refer to this handbook whenever an employee shows signs of poor job performance. Whatever the source of the problem—whether it stems from use of alcohol or other drugs, or from family, marital, financial or general health problems—it can be handled by using the five steps detailed in this book.

INTRODUCTION
Making Successful Employees:
What's in It for You?

WHAT'S THE PROBLEM?

You are a busy person. Now your boss or employee assistance director expects you to take time to complete this workbook. Why? Is it just more paper pushing? Or is it something that can produce real benefits for you and your department?

To find out why, complete the following true/false questions. Your answers will show specific ways in which you and your company can benefit by dealing effectively with problem employees.

WHY REFER PROBLEM EMPLOYEES?

Circle T for True or F for False.

1. If you could increase productivity by ten to thirty percent *without hiring new people*, your company would appreciate or reward this improvement.   T   F

2. If health costs in your department were significantly decreased, this savings would reflect well on departmental efficiency.   T   F

3. Less absenteeism would permit smoother flow of production and cut down overtime.   T   F

4. Reducing the number of accidents in any department would show good supervision and employee cooperation with company safety efforts.   T   F

---

5. Decreasing mistakes and downtime would increase productivity and decrease operating costs. It would also make happier customers.   T   F

6. Employee turnover costs the company thousands of dollars to hire and train new people. Keeping qualified employees on the payroll longer promotes loyalty, consistency, and productivity.   T   F

7. When one employee has a personal problem, it can affect the whole department's morale. When morale goes down, so does productivity.   T   F

The correct answer to all seven questions is True.

Although statistics vary according to departments and companies, here are the startling facts that correspond to each numbered question above:

1. From 10 to 23 percent of any work force is using alcohol or other drugs.[1] These figures *include your company and even your department*. Even when employees appear to be "normal," they can be using alcohol or other drugs, thereby significantly decreasing departmental productivity because of poor decision making and non-creative work.[2]

2. Alcohol and other drugs cost U.S. industry more than $100 billion a year. For instance, the chemically dependent employee uses three times the normal level of sick

---

[1] National Institute on Drug Abuse, *Strategic Planning for Workplace Drug Abuse Programs*, U.S. Department of Health and Human Services, Public Health Service; Alcohol, Drug Abuse, and Mental Health Administration; Office for Research Communications: Rockville, MD, 1987, p. 4.
[2] NIDA, op cit.

benefits. The disease of chemical dependence may account directly or indirectly for over half of the medical claims filed by employees and their families.[3]

3. Employees who use alcohol or other drugs arrive late at work three times more often and lose twice as much work. They are absent 2.5 times more often for periods of eight days or longer.[4]

4. Employees who use alcohol or other drugs become involved in accidents 3.6 to 5 times more often than other employees.[5] Drinking or using on the job drastically impairs reflex action, hand/eye coordination, memory, and judgment.[6]

5. One airline computer operator, impaired by marijuana, forgot to load a vital tape. The reservation system went down for eight hours, costing the company $19 million.[7] Less dramatic mistakes happen every day in your department.

6. The use of alcohol or other drugs is a significant predictor of job change or loss, even when other factors are considered.[8] With today's scarcity of qualified employees, rehabilitation makes more sense than termination.

---

[3] Milt Freudenheim, "More Aid for Addicts on the Job," *The New York Times*, November 13, 1989, p. D1.
[4] NIDA, op cit.
[5] Freudenheim, op cit., p. D4.
[6] J. Michael Walsh and Steven W. Gust, "Drug Abuse in the Workplace: Issues, Policy Decisions, and Corporate Response," National Institute on Drug Abuse: Rockville, MD, 1987, p. 239.
[7] NIDA, op cit.
[8] Walsh and Gust, op cit., p. 237.

7. Other employees may resent the problem employee's lateness, lack of responsibility, or hostile attitude. Or, they may cover up his or her actions. Some will do the problem employee's work, overload themselves, and make mistakes; others will adopt the problem employee's sloppy work habits. Normal employees may worry about their personal safety and security when working with an employee who uses alcohol or other drugs.

These facts show how this workbook can help you. It can help eliminate one of the biggest drains on your energy, time, and resources: the problem employee. This employee's poor work performance may be caused by use of alcohol or other drugs. It may stem from physical, emotional, or mental problems that need professional help. Or it may come from financial, family, or marital stresses that carry over into the workplace. Solving these problems goes beyond the scope of the manager or supervisor's job. Instead, the problem employee should be *referred* to the appropriate company or community resource.

Your referral helps turn a problem employee into a success. *It stops the problem from getting worse and starts the process of recovery.*

Remember, you are the most important person in the referral process. You can make a difference, not only in your department, but in the lives of your employees. And that is not just paper pushing.

SUPERVISOR'S OBJECTIVES FOR COMPLETING THIS WORKBOOK

Now that you better understand the purpose of this book, you can set some objectives that you want to achieve. Check the objectives below that seem most important to you at this point.

By completing this workbook, I will:

_____ Recognize problem employees in my department.

_____ Increase departmental productivity.

_____ Decrease health-related costs.

_____ Improve departmental morale.

_____ Learn how to refer problem employees to appropriate company and community resources.

_____ Learn how to protect myself when problem employees resist referral.

_____ Recognize how my own behavior may interfere with the problem employee's finding help.

_____ Focus my time, energy, and talent more on doing my job, and less on solving other people's problems.

_____ Other _____

When you have completed this book, look back and see how well you have accomplished your objectives.

STEP ONE
Documenting: An Essential Supervisory Skill

Turning negative statistics into positive productivity begins with referral. Remember, "referral" may be defined as follows:

Referral is using company and community resources to assess problems and recommend solutions that will improve employee performance.

When managers and supervisors observe an employee who has a job performance problem, they should *not*:
1) try to diagnose the cause of the problem;
2) assume that the employee is using alcohol or other drugs;
3) ignore the problem.

Instead, to respect the employee's rights—*and to protect yourself from possible legal action by the employee, the union, or the Equal Employment Opportunity Commission—all referrals must be based on documented evidence.*

Careful documentation cannot be successfully challenged. In the event that you or your company faces litigation, you will have sufficient written evidence to support your referral.

Strictly Confidential!

All documentation must be kept *strictly confidential* to avoid invading the employee's privacy and to defend against possible legal action.

Documentation can be kept confidential by following these suggestions:

1. Keep all documentation separate from general files or personnel records.
2. Keep all documentation in a locked file.
3. Assign a code or number to the employee's file and refer to the employee only by that code or number, not by name.
4. Use a confidential coding system to record incidents. For instance:
   - Mark individual time sheets with color-coded pencils.
   - Mark your appointment calendar with a coded letter or number.
   - Write notations on a numbered sheet in a locked file.
   - Put your comments on your computer and protect the information with a confidential access code.
5. Never discuss the employee with anyone except a representative of your company's Employee Assistance Program or other person to whom you are referring the employee.

Document Facts. Do Not Diagnose.

Documentation should include facts covering these four points:

1. Who was involved.
2. What happened.
3. When and where the incident occurred.
4. Witnesses, if any.

Document every incident *without diagnosing the cause*. For instance, the following documentation is *not correctly written*:

"She looked drunk."

This is not correct because it diagnoses the employee's behavior as alcoholic intoxication. In fact, the employee's behavior can have a non-alcohol-related cause, such as fatigue, illness, or use of prescribed medications.

Correctly written documentation observes the facts, without diagnosing. The following examples are *correctly written*:

"She slurred her speech."

"She staggered from her desk to the ladies room."

"She knocked her lamp off her desk."
"She threw her coffee cup at the copy machine."

WRITING DOCUMENTATION

Read the following case studies, then decide which documentation is correctly or incorrectly written.

Case 1: Johnny. On Monday, Johnny, an experienced warehouse employee, dropped a case of canned goods and injured his foot. Two days later, he knocked over a shelf of boxed cookies, damaging most of the inventory. Today, he fell off the loading dock and cut his leg.

Indicate what statements are correctly written by writing C for Correct and I for Incorrect.

_____ 1. "Johnny must have been drunk."

_____ 2. "Johnny hurt his foot."

_____ 3. "He dropped a case of canned goods and injured his right foot."

_____ 4. "He looked like he was high on something."

_____ 5. "Wednesday, about 11:30 a.m., he fell off the loading dock and cut his left leg. Martin witnessed the incident and helped him to the nurse's office."

Answers: Documentation 1, 2, and 4 are *not correct*. Number 1 diagnoses the problem as alcoholic intoxication. Number 2 uses the employee's name. Number 4 is too vague an observation and makes a diagnosis. Numbers 3 and 5 are correctly written; both document specific facts about the incident.

Case 2: Janet. Janet is a neat, polite, conscientious young woman who was recently promoted to customer service representative. Two weeks ago, a customer complained that Janet had promised to deliver the replacement for a damaged part, but she failed to show up or even telephone. Last Thursday, you noticed that Janet arrived late to work, appeared disheveled and flustered, and disappeared for over an hour, without telling anyone where she was going. Today, she fell asleep in the weekly departmental meeting.

Indicate what statements are correctly written by writing C for Correct and I for Incorrect.

_____ 1. "Thursday 5/21, Employee A arrived at 9:23, 23 minutes late."

_____ 2. "Thursday morning she looked like she had a bad hangover."

_____ 3. "5/7, received telephone complaint from Mr. Stevens at Consolidated. Employee A failed to deliver part as promised."

_____ 4. "I'm sure she's drinking on the job."

_____ 5. "She fell asleep at today's 9 a.m. meeting. Martha had to wake her up."

Answers: Numbers 1, 3, and 5 are *correctly written*. Number 2 is not a factual observation. A better way to state how a person looks is to give exact observations, such as, "Her eyes were red and her face appeared puffy." Number 4 makes a diagnosis which may or may not be correct.

Case 3: Your department. Think about your department. Visualize each person's *normal* appearance and behavior. Have you noticed any employee whose appearance or behavior has changed in the past month? Any performance problems? Difficulty getting along with others? Write your observations about this employee's work performance below:

_____

_____

_____

_____

_____

_____

_____

_____

_____

_____

Check to make sure your documentation *observes, but does not diagnose.* Make sure you noted date, time, place, persons present, and a brief description of any incident.

In the future, you might use the following form to make sure you have correctly documented behavior which may indicate that an employee should be referred.

SAMPLE DOCUMENTATION FORM

Employee's Code _____

Date/Time _____

Place _____

Physical Appearance _____

_____

_____

_____

Others Present _____

_____

_____

_____

Description of Incident _____

_____

_____

_____

_____

Your Action at That Time _____

_____

_____

_____

_____

Three Important Points to Remember:
1. **Supervisors observe, they do not diagnose.**
2. **Supervisors document, they do not guess.**
3. **Supervisors refer, they do not counsel.**

STEP TWO
Identifying Problem Employees

The basic concept of referral is this: **Referral is based on the employee's work performance.** If your department is running smoothly and all employees are performing well, you have no problem. No problem, no referral.

However, just because you don't *see* a problem doesn't mean there isn't one. Someone in your department may be causing subtle problems that affect productivity. For instance, an employee's bad attitude can undermine morale and make productivity suffer. Before you can find the solution, you must locate the problem.

ANY SIGNS OF A PROBLEM?

Circle yes or no for each of the following questions:

1. Are you aware of any employee who may have a problem that is affecting his or her job performance?   Yes No

2. Are you secretly worried about a certain employee in your department?   Yes No

3. Have you talked or complained about a certain employee?   Yes No

4. Have others talked or complained about a certain employee?   Yes No

5. Close your eyes and visualize each employee in your department. Do you think your department would run more smoothly if that person were not there?   Yes No

---

Any yes answer is a sign that you may have a problem employee in your department. Here are other signs of actual or potential problem employees who may be damaging your department's productivity.

WHAT IS THE PROBLEM?

Check any of the following situations that presently apply to your department or area.

____Drugs are missing from a supply cabinet.

____Your department seems to be constantly behind schedule.

____There is a crisis orientation in the department; things do not operate smoothly.

____Customers have complained about lack of service, poor products, or rudeness.

____Experienced employees do not want to work with a particular employee.

____One person constantly seems to cause trouble.

____Arguments break out unexpectedly.

____The team is not functioning as a unit.

____Lack of communication permeates the entire department.

____Few employees seem enthusiastic.

____Work is piling up. Too many accidents are giving the department a poor rating.

____Sloppy work is increasing the number of rejected products or returns.

____Insurance paperwork is increasing.

____A security investigation is underway in your division or department.

____Resignations outnumber those in other departments. Turnover is high.

____Plum assignments are going to other departments.

____Your competition is winning.

____Describe any other situations in your department that concern you.

_____

_____

_____

There may be many explanations for these problems. One likely explanation is that you have an employee who has a problem with alcohol or other drugs, or who has other problems that affect work quality. "But," you may ask, "how can one person cause all that trouble?"

Impact on Your Department

An employee who uses alcohol or other drugs, or who has another problem that affects work performance, can ravage a department in a short period. Serious departmental problems may be developing right now, without your being aware that a problem employee is in your midst.

Here are some ways the problem employee can undermine your department. Check any of the following situations you have observed:

____ 1. The problem employee's attitude—whether it is hostile, suspicious, self-pitying, or dishonest—spreads dissatisfaction among other employees. Other employees begin to complain, slough responsibility, or argue among themselves. Morale droops. Work quality suffers.

____ 2. The problem employee may become less responsible and fail to contribute to the team effort; as a result, others may feel compelled to step in and do his or her job. Or the problem employee may become grandiose, try to take control, and leave other employees feeling resentful.

____ 3. Sometimes, co-workers cover up the problem employee's mistakes or offer excuses for absences. This behavior is called "enabling," and allows the problem to continue and grow.

____ 4. In other cases, co-workers may refuse to work with a problem employee, causing a rift in departmental relationships.

____ 5. Problem employees—and the co-workers they hurt—take their problems home. Stress increases marital and family discord, and it boosts the number of health claims from your department. As insurance costs rise, departmental efficiency drops. Your reputation as a "hot" department can cool, and you can begin to lose challenging assignments to more productive groups.

Through these and many other ways, problem employees can ruin departments. The remedy is identifying and referring problem employees to the appropriate company resource in a timely, fair, confidential, and legal manner.

In some cases, the whole department may need referral to the EAP or outside consultant. For instance, every employee may need training to identify the signs of chemical dependence and to increase awareness of the company's programs and benefits. Or human relations problems may indicate that everyone needs training to improve communication skills and build team spirit. In such cases, referral can bring positive changes throughout the department.

Who Is the Problem?

If you checked any of the problems or concerns listed above, you probably have at least one problem employee in your midst, and possibly more. Your first task is to find out *who the problem employee is.*

Five methods for identifying a problem employee are:
1. Set work performance standards.
2. Observe changes in behavior.
3. Notice signs of family problems.
4. Analyze complaints.
5. Spot departmental "red flags."

Method 1: Set Work Performance Standards

Performance standards for each job give supervisors specific guidelines for identifying employees who are not working up to par. They also provide helpful information for performance reviews. Performance standards detail *how work should be executed* and *how performance will be measured.*

Work performance standards differ according to each employee's job; for instance, a nurse on a hospital day shift must meet far different standards than a city bus operator. But *standards should be the same for all employees in the same job type.*

Work performance standards should include both tangible and intangible measures.

Tangible work performance standards are measurable. These might include speed, accuracy, and punctuality. Here is an example of a tangible work performance standard based on punctuality:

"An employee is considered 'on time' if he or she punches the time clock within five minutes of the start of the assigned shift."

Intangible work performance standards are more difficult to measure, but they are often more important to overall departmental functioning. These may include cooperativeness, enthusiasm, and creativity. Here is an example of an intangible work performance standard based on cooperativeness:

"All employees are expected to cooperate by completing their part of the job on schedule."

These tangible and intangible work performance standards give you a way to measure poor, adequate, or superior performance. *Only when you can give specific examples of poor performance do you have a clear case for referring a problem employee.*

TANGIBLE OR INTANGIBLE?

Identify whether a work performance standard is tangible or intangible by writing T for Tangible and I for Intangible in the space provided.

_____ 1. enthusiasm
_____ 2. respect for authority
_____ 3. dexterity
_____ 4. compassion
_____ 5. production output
_____ 6. meeting sales quotas
_____ 7. number and duration of work breaks
_____ 8. friendliness
_____ 9. attending required meetings
_____ 10. courtesy

(Answers: 1-I, 2-I, 3-T, 4-I, 5-T, 6-T, 7-T, 8-I, 9-T, 10-I.)

Written job descriptions are different than written work performance standards. Job descriptions tell employees *what* they should do. Work performance standards tell them *how* they should do it; they take *quality* of performance into account.

Both tangible and intangible performance standards should be *written* so that each employee knows what you expect. These can be written in easy-to-understand "generic" terms that convey a general idea of standards that apply to all job descriptions.

The following are examples of "generic" work performance standards:

1. Maintains an acceptable attendance record.
2. Performs all duties at a competent level.
3. Gets along well with co-workers and customers.
4. Maintains acceptable level of productivity (sales, output).
5. Contributes to overall department success.
6. Shows interest in job and willingness to contribute.

WRITING GENERIC WORK PERFORMANCE STANDARDS

Here is a generic work performance standard based on productivity:

"Meets production requirements."

In the space below, write a generic work performance standard for *accuracy*. Then check your version against the suggested wordings below.

_____

_____

Here is a generic work performance standard based on courtesy:

"Treats co-workers and customers courteously."

In the space below, write a generic work performance standard for *attitude*. Then check your version against the suggested wordings below.

Examples of suggested wordings:
Accuracy:
    "Completes work with acceptable accuracy."
    "Maintains good accuracy."
Attitude:
    "Keeps a positive attitude."
    "Shows an attitude of cooperation."

As time permits, say, over six months, you might write specific work performance standards for each job description. You might form a three- or four-person team or invite selected employee representatives to form an *ad hoc* committee to write and approve work performance standards. A union representative can participate on the committee. With specific work performance standards for each job, you have clear guidelines for identifying below-par performance and referring a problem employee.

Method 2: Observe Changes in Behavior

A second way to identify problem employees is by observing changes in their behavior. For instance:

- A usually cheerful, friendly sales representative may turn sullen and withdrawn.
- An ordinarily punctual, hard-working engineer may begin arriving late and leaving early.
- A technician known for her accuracy may become mistake-prone.

Changes in attitude, mood, work habits, accuracy, and productivity are "red flags" for supervisors.

"Red flags" are warning signs that a change has taken place that affects the employee's output. This change may be caused by such factors as:

- *general health*; for instance, the employee may have a cold or flu that is causing fatigue and inattentiveness.
- *personal, family, financial, or marital problems* that keep the employee unfocused.
- *on-the-job concerns,* such as the employee's feelings of inadequacy in the face of a difficult assignment.

Whatever the reason, the change marks a departure from the norm. Still, action may not be required. The illness, distraction, or emotional interference may evaporate in a few days. However, if behavior changes persist for more than a few days, you will have to take action and begin documentation to support any referral you might make.

Method 3. Notice Signs of Family Problems

As a supervisor, you probably prefer to stay out of your employees' personal lives. You rightly believe that their off-the-job activities are none of your business. Yet sometimes their personal lives intrude into their work lives, and their output drops. Then it is your business.

You may notice increasing signs of family problems, that is, family tension, discord, or illness. Here are some examples. Check any that are similar to situations that have occurred in your department or that presently concern you.

_____A male employee tells you that his teenage son ran away from home or spent the night in jail.

_____Another employee complains that his eight-year-old is failing reading class.

_____A female employee mentions recurring financial worries.

_____Personnel reports that Joe has filed six health claims for his children this month.

_____Another employee confides that Jill had to take a second job, move to a less expensive apartment, and take her children out of private school.

_____A male employee is having serious marital problems.

Examples like these are more red flags, signals that some deeply disturbing problem is putting additional stress on an employee's family.

While every family has problems, many families can work together and find solutions. But some families do not have the relationship or communication skills to deal with their problems. They may be disrupted by a member who uses alcohol or other drugs. Or they may be unable to solve long-standing financial or health problems. Therefore, family problems keep growing and may eventually invade the workplace.

When family problems distract the employee from his or her job, the manager or supervisor may be the only person clearheaded enough to take corrective action. The trained manager or supervisor will be able to refer the employee to resources that can help families in crisis.

Again, these observations must be documented in order to be of value in the referral process.

Method 4. Analyze Complaints

Another method for identifying problem employees is listening to and noting complaints from other employees. Complaints may stem from sudden changes in a co-worker's behavior that jeopardize the safety and welfare of other persons. Here is one example:

A nursing supervisor became alarmed when one of her night nurses complained that another nurse, who was usually kind and considerate, was verbally abusing elderly patients and refusing to help them get from the bed to the bathroom. When another nurse complained that the abusive nurse had angrily pushed her, the supervisor knew that a problem employee had surfaced.

In addition to complaints arising from an employee's behavior changes, other complaints may arise from relationship problems. Check any of the following examples of relationship problems that seem similar to those in your department:

_____An employee's anger builds up and explodes unexpectedly.

_____An employee throws insults or verbal barbs at inopportune times.

____An employee habitually shirks responsibility.
____An employee has a superior attitude.
____An employee continually withdraws (isolates) from others in
the department.
____Other employees gossip about an employee.
____Other employees want an employee transferred.

As with behavior changes and family problems, you must document these relationship complaints for referral purposes.

Method 5. Spot Departmental Red Flags

While you may not notice changes in an individual employee's behavior, be aware of family stress, or hear employee complaints, you can quickly notice slips in departmental productivity. For example:
- In your daily review of your department's performance, you can instantly spot a drop in output, sales, deliveries, or customers.
- By reading reports, you can analyze subtle declines in the quality of your product or service.
- By listening carefully at meetings, you can pick up clues to the causes of lower motivation.
- Being alert for changes, you can become aware of missed deadlines, increasing accidents or absenteeism, or a general malaise infecting your department.

These red flags may point to an employee who is using alcohol or other drugs, or who needs professional help.

Several sources of information will help you spot these red flags:
- sales reports
- attendance records
- overtime reports
- health claims
- competitive activity
- customer complaints
- cost-per-sale
- overhead

Study such reports with this question in mind:
Do these figures indicate a problem employee in my department?

You may be surprised to learn that trends point not to a general or seasonal downturn but to a problem employee who is affecting productivity and morale.

List Information Sources
List below all documents, such as sales, attendance, inventory, and overtime reports, that give you information regarding departmental effectiveness. Include reports of competitive sales, as well as summaries from the personnel and health departments.

_____

_____

_____

_____

_____

Looking at your list of information resources above, circle Yes or No to answer this question:
Am I utilizing these resources to identify problem employees?   Yes   No

If you answer no, make a commitment to analyze these reports more closely. One report may not tell the whole story, but comparing figures may reveal a hidden problem. For instance, your overtime report may show that two employees are adding up excessive hours, yet sales summaries show no increase to warrant overtime. This red flag may mean that a problem employee is not performing adequately, forcing the other two employees to work extra hours to get the job done.

Identifying problem employees is a skill that requires observation and analysis.   As part of your on-going responsibilities, you will find that these skills take only a few minutes of your time, yet pay big dividends in increased departmental productivity.

❖   ❖   ❖

REVIEW
Look back at the five methods for identifying problem employees explained in this chapter. Check the ones you will use in your department.
_____ 1. Set work performance standards.
_____ 2. Observe changes in behavior.
_____ 3. Notice signs of family problems.
_____ 4. Analyze complaints.
_____ 5. Analyze departmental "red flags."

STEP THREE
Eliminating Enabling: The Principal Barrier to Referral

Many managers and supervisors are reluctant to refer employees, even if they suspect that an employee is chemically dependent (that is, dependent on alcohol or other drugs). There are many reasons for their reluctance.

REASONS FOR RELUCTANCE TO REFER

Check any reasons that may apply to you.

____ You don't want to make a diagnosis or "moral judgment."

____ You feel uncomfortable confronting a problem employee.

____ You believe you should solve the problem yourself.

____ You would rather fire the person and get rid of the problem permanently.

____ You think a "good" manager or supervisor keeps problems within the department and does not "blow the whistle" on valued employees.

____ You think the problem is only temporary and not serious enough to warrant the time and paperwork involved in referral.

____ You believe there's nothing wrong with drinking alcohol or using other drugs on the job. In fact, you sometimes do it yourself.

Reasons like these can create a barrier that prevents problem employees from getting the help they need. This barrier is called *enabling*.

Enabling is a complex pattern of ideas, feelings, attitudes, and behaviors that allows alcohol or other drug problems to continue by preventing the employee from facing the consequences of his or her actions.

When an employee has a problem with alcohol or other drugs, enabling behavior is a barrier to referral—and a barrier to recovery—because it permits poor work performance and allows the employee's problem to continue.

Enablers may include:
- managers and supervisors
- co-workers
- clients or customers
- suppliers or service persons
- friends and family members

People become enablers by such actions as:
- failing to enforce the company's policies concerning alcohol and other drugs
- covering up an employee's mistakes
- making excuses for an employee's behavior
- avoiding dealing with an employee because of his or her sex
- avoiding meeting or working with an employee
- ignoring evidence of declining work performance
- refusing to listen to co-workers' complaints about an employee
- doing a problem employee's work or assuming his or her other responsibilities
- failing to document unusual behavior or work performance problems
- excusing an employee's verbally abusive language
- counseling the employee, rather than referring to EAP
- refusing to believe that a valued employee or personal friend could have a problem with alcohol or other drugs
- failing to take disciplinary action

- keeping the company's EAP or human resources professionals uninformed
- avoiding writing work performance standards
- rationalizing that the employee's mistake, accident, or outburst is a one-time happening
- drinking alcohol or using other drugs at work
- encouraging the use of alcohol or other drugs in work-related situations, such as company parties or conventions

Enablers usually act unconsciously. That is, they are often unaware that they are enabling. They may believe they are helping the chemically dependent person or being a good friend. Enabling may have positive payoffs; that is, it may make the supervisor feel kind, generous, safe, or even superior. Consequently, enabling is extremely difficult to recognize in one's self and even more difficult to stop.

On the following page is an exercise that can help you decide whether or not you are an enabler.

CHECKLIST: ARE YOU AN ENABLER?

Are you unknowingly permitting an employee to continue unproductive, disruptive, or destructive behavior in your department? To find out, use the following checklist of enabling actions. Check any actions you made during the past four weeks.

_____ I advanced money to an employee for a second or third time.

_____ I lied about or did not convey my concerns about a problem employee to my superior or other managers or supervisors.

_____ I explained to my superior how a mistake or accident happened, without naming the person who caused it.

_____ I avoided coming into contact with a problem employee.

_____ I spent too much time thinking and worrying about a problem employee.

_____ I accepted an employee's excuse for poor performance without checking the facts.

_____ I made excuses for an employee's rudeness, lateness, or incompetence.

_____ I took over an employee's responsibilities.

_____ I allowed an employee to yell at or insult me or someone else.

_____ I felt guilty or angry because I spent too much time trying to supervise an employee.

_____ I asked other employees to be more understanding about "poor Joe's" problems.

_____ I felt pity and sympathy for an employee's personal problems.

_____ I tried to solve an employee's personal problems by counseling or advising.

_____ I said yes when I wanted to say no.

_____ I felt guilty or angry because an employee got into trouble.

_____ I lowered work performance standards for an employee.

_____ I observed on-the-job use of alcohol or other drugs, but said nothing to the employee or anyone else.

_____ I insisted to my superior that none of my employees had a problem with alcohol or other drugs, even though I thought otherwise.

_____ I did not report an employee's poor work performance because I was afraid it would reflect badly on my supervisory ability.

_____ I overlooked or ignored an employee's talking about having a hangover.

_____ I gossiped about an employee's use of alcohol or other drugs.

If you checked one or more of these actions, you are probably an enabler. Being an enabler does not mean that you are a thoughtless person or an ineffective supervisor. Nor does it mean that you should blame yourself or feel guilty because an employee has work performance problems due to alcohol or other drugs. It means that you need to understand the disease of chemical dependence and learn more about the consequences of enabling in the workplace.

BREAKING THE ENABLING PATTERN

Here are some suggestions for breaking your own enabling pattern, as well as enabling patterns that may be evident among your employees or throughout the company. Check the ones you think will work best.

_____ Learn more about the problem of alcohol and other drugs in the workplace.

_____ Be honest about a problem employee's behavior.

_____ Use the checklist above to review your actions and decisions at the end of each day.

_____ Write work performance standards for each job description.

_____ Begin documenting poor work performance for all employees.

_____ Ask the Employee Assistance Department to conduct a department-wide educational program on enabling.

_____ Discuss your personal experiences with alcohol or other drugs with a knowledgeable professional.

_____ Take a firm stand against the use of alcohol or other drugs in company-sponsored events.

_____ Learn more about the company's policies concerning alcohol and other drugs, and make a commitment to enforce those policies.

_____ Support those employees who are involved in a recovery program.

_____ Cooperate with other managers and supervisors who are trying to change company policies concerning alcohol and other drugs.

_____ Suggest a program of counseling for problem employees.

_____ Examine honestly your feelings toward employees who have problems with alcohol or other drugs.

_____ Discuss your concerns about a problem employee with your immediate superior.

_____ Stop suggesting by words or actions that you approve of the use of alcohol or other drugs on the job.

Now choose *one* of the suggestions you checked above and *do it*. Make a telephone call. Set up an appointment. Write a memo. Call a meeting. Make a list. Post a notice on the department bulletin board. Re-read company policies. Your decisive action can start a chain reaction of positive steps to counteract enabling throughout the company.

Reasons for Enabling

There are a number of reasons for enabling. These reasons create barriers that prevent referral. Understanding these reasons helps you become aware of your actions and make necessary changes. Five common reasons for enabling are:

1. Personal attitudes about alcohol and other drugs.
2. Denial and minimizing.
3. Fear of being disliked or appearing incompetent.
4. Unwillingness to disrupt the work schedule.
5. Distrust of health care professionals.

Reason 1: Personal attitude about alcohol and other drugs

Managers and supervisors may unconsciously bring to the workplace attitudes from childhood, from previous work experience, or from their own use of alcohol or other drugs. These attitudes may prevent them from referring problem employees. No matter how competent these managers and supervisors may be, their reluctance to make a referral can decrease departmental efficiency.

Drug-permissive environment. You may have grown up or worked in a drug-permissive environment. Your parents or other family members, friends, or co-workers may have used alcohol or other drugs; consequently, you may now believe that such behavior is "normal" or "harmless."

The ways people use alcohol and other drugs range from experimental and recreational use to high-frequency, high-level compulsive use.[9] However, *any level of use* detracts from a person's

---

[9] Richard Seymour and David E. Smith. *Drugfree,* New York: Facts on File Publications, 1987, p. 16.

ability to sustain peak work performance. If employees are drinking or using on the job, *their performance is cut by at least one-third*. The use of alcohol and other drugs, no matter at what level, really is not "harmless" after all.

Negative past experiences. Your past experiences influence your attitudes about alcohol and other drugs. These attitudes may contribute to enabling and prevent referral. Here are a few examples.

Check any of these negative experiences that seem similar to your own past experiences.

_____Your parents or other significant adults may have had religious beliefs that condemned alcoholics or other chemically dependent people. You may now carry those same beliefs into the workplace.

_____One or both of your parents may have used alcohol or other drugs; if, due to that use, they were verbally or physically abusive to each other or to you, your unhappy memories may influence your attitudes today.

_____You may have worked with a chemically dependent person whose destructive behavior affected your job; now you feel suspicious of anyone whose behavior indicates a possible problem with alcohol or other drugs.

_____You may have become distrustful of people who are recovering from chemical dependence because of their tendency to return to drinking or using.

For these or other reasons, you may now hold negative feelings toward *all* people who are chemically dependent. These feelings may have built barriers to referring problem employees.

Today, health care professionals know that alcohol and other drug dependence is a *disease*. Like diabetes or arthritis, it can be diagnosed, treated, and arrested. When you refer a possible chemically dependent person, a health care professional will assess the problem and recommend appropriate counseling or treatment. The recovering chemically dependent person has a much better chance of staying clean and sober when supervisors and managers take appropriate, informed action.

Personal use of alcohol or other drugs. Managers and supervisors sometimes have a personal problem with alcohol or other drugs that they are afraid to recognize.

- If they are drinking alcohol or using other drugs excessively, they may think other people's addictive behavior is "normal" because they act the same way.
- They may ignore an employee's problem because they believe their own drinking or using has no effect on their work performance.
- They may be afraid that referring a problem employee will call attention to their personal use of alcohol or other drugs; therefore, they keep quiet.

These managers and supervisors have the option to self-refer. *Self-referral* accounts for over thirty percent of the new clients in many employee assistance programs. They can make an appointment with one of the company's employee assistance or human resources professionals. During that appointment, the professional will assess the problem, explain company benefits, and initiate a counseling or treatment plan. Because of company policies that protect anonymity, managers and supervisors can seek help without jeopardizing their career.

If the company does not provide employee assistance benefits, managers and supervisors can look in the city classified directory under "Alcoholism," "Drug Abuse Information," or "Employee Assistance Programs." They can make an appointment to talk to an outside counselor or treatment facility.

Reason 2: Denial and minimizing

Managers and supervisors often believe that their department is "squeaky clean." That is, they believe use of alcohol or other drugs may occur in *other* departments, but not in theirs. Often they handpick their employees and know enough about each one to insist that no one is chemically dependent. On the other hand, they may be closing their eyes to a problem that is clearly evident to everyone else. This head-in-the-sand attitude is called *denial*. Because of denial, a lot of chemically dependent people do not get treatment and continue to suffer.

Here is a definition of denial:

Denial claims that nothing is wrong when something obviously is.

Here is an example of denial:

A supervisor received a report that a long-time employee had been arrested for DWI (Driving While Intoxicated) and lost his license for three months. Because that employee's job required driving, the supervisor knew that he should temporarily reassign the employee to a non-driving job. However, the employee loudly claimed that he had drunk "only two beers" and that the arresting officer "had it in for me." The supervisor sympathized and agreed that "there must be some mistake" and allowed the employee to continue driving without a license.

This extreme example shows why denial is dangerous. The manager or supervisor who is *in denial* . . .

- refuses to face reality and take appropriate steps
- damages the employee's chances to get help
- reflects badly on his or her decision-making ability
- indicates to other employees that excessive drinking is okay
- endangers public safety

Minimizing is similar to denial. When a manager or supervisor makes a problem appear less serious than it really is, that person is minimizing. Minimizing includes:

- covering up the extent of a problem
- making it seem less important than other problems
- becoming so accustomed to a problem that it seems "normal"
- telling others, such as employees and other managers and supervisors, not to "make a big deal out of it" or blow things out of proportion

---

IDENTIFYING DENIAL AND MINIMIZING

Are you *in denial* about an employee in your department? Are you *minimizing* an employee's problem with alcohol or other drugs? To find out, check any of the following comments that you have recently said:

____ "He's just having a bad day."
____ "She'll straighten herself out."
____ "Joe's not that kind of guy."
____ "I'm sure it won't happen again."
____ "I've known her for years. She wouldn't do such a thing."
____ "It wasn't *that* serious."
____ "Everyone's making a big deal out of nothing."
____ "It's not as bad as what happened in (Sid's) department."

If you have said any of these or similar things, think for a few moments about the employee you were discussing. Then ask yourself these questions:

- Does his or her work meet performance standards?
- Was his or her behavior uncharacteristic?
- Have you heard complaints or seen "red flags" that may indicate a problem with this employee?
- How often have you minimized this employee's behavior?

The way to overcome your own tendency to minimize is to document each incident as it happens. No matter how small the incident, write it down. In a week or two, review the facts and evaluate the evidence. Either there is a problem, or there isn't. If there is, you can stop denying and start referring.

Reason 3: Fear of being disliked or appearing incompetent

Some managers and supervisors fear that referring problem employees will make them unpopular with other employees. Yet the opposite is usually true.

Employees appreciate a department where they get fair treatment, where they can do their best, and where their rights are honored. They feel unfairly treated when a problem employee continues to disrupt the entire department and doesn't fulfill his or her portion of the workload. They feel frustrated when their own work is undermined by someone who has a problem with alcohol or other drugs. They believe they have the right to work in a safe, stable environment, and they appreciate the manager or supervisor who protects that right.

When managers and supervisors refer a problem employee, some employees may not like the immediate results. One reason is that, if a co-worker takes a leave of absence, other employees may have to pick up the slack. While employees may not like the extra work load, they will like the smoother, more pleasant atmosphere of a department no longer affected by an employee's alcohol or other drug use.

Some managers and supervisors fear appearing incompetent. They unconsciously fear that referring a problem employee will reflect badly on their problem-solving ability. As a result, they may try to be an all-around marriage counselor, family therapist, financial advisor, and chemical dependence counselor for their department. Obviously, these functions are outside the scope of managerial or supervisory responsibilities.

The fear of appearing incompetent may be deeply imbedded in your unconscious. It may stem from abusive criticism in your childhood or from other early experiences. It may cause such unpleasant feelings of shame, vulnerability, and weakness that you avoid it at any cost. You may even avoid associating with people whom you consider incompetent.

When this fear blocks referral, a manager or supervisor may want to consider ways to deal with personal issues; for example, getting some personal counseling. Understanding the source of fear can help managers manage more effectively.

Reason 4: Unwillingness to disrupt the work schedule

Many managers and supervisors are reluctant to take an employee off the job because production might slow down. As a result, the problem employee stays, even when his or her behavior is disruptive.

True, *unplanned absences* can throw the entire department off schedule. But *planned absences* can be arranged to minimize the impact on production.

After assessing the employee's problem, the EAP may recommend financial, marital, or family counseling. Such sessions can be scheduled outside regular work hours so that they do not interfere with deadlines. Or, the EAP may recommend treatment for chemical dependence. In this case, the manager or supervisor can reassign employees to make sure all shifts are covered, or they can hire a temporary person for the specific period that treatment takes the employee off the job. Production need not suffer.

PLANNING AHEAD TO MEET PRODUCTION

How can you plan ahead when you refer problem employees? Here are some suggestions. Check those that would work best in your company.

____ 1. Assign other personnel to cover the time slot.
____ 2. Fill in for the employee yourself.
____ 3. Require the employee to come in an hour earlier or leave an hour later.
____ 4. Arrange the employee's absence for slowest periods.
____ 5. Hire a temporary person to cover the absence.
____ 6. Give the employee the responsibility for completing his or her work at a future time.
____ 7. Work out a plan with the employee.
____ 8. Re-schedule regular meetings.

Describe here any other method you have used to plan for an employee's absence.

_____

_____

_____

_____

Reason 5: Distrust of health care professionals

Some managers and supervisors may distrust professional counselors and therapists. Therefore, they resist referring problem employees.

Here are some of the reasons managers and supervisors may distrust health care professionals. Check any reasons that are similar to your own.

_____ Managers and supervisors may have had disappointing experiences with counselors in the past; consequently, they now think that all counselors are unqualified.

_____ They may resent the high cost of counseling or treatment, or they may resent someone else's "interference" in their employee's affairs.

_____ They may believe that a problem employee can "straighten himself out" if he just "sets his mind to it." Because of these beliefs, the same manager or supervisor who would readily refer an injured employee to the medical department will refuse to refer a problem employee to the EAP.

_____ Some managers and supervisors believe that counselors and therapists give problem employees too much sympathy ("They're just hanky-passers," says one supervisor.) They consider this hand-holding approach too soft.

If you checked any of the reasons above, you might want to consider this fact: **You leave yourself few options when you distrust health care professionals.**

What are your options? One option is to threaten a problem employee with dismissal, but that strategy rarely works. Instead, it causes the employee to become more secretive. If chemical dependence is the underlying problem, the employee soon becomes more clever at concealing the use of alcohol or other drugs.

Another option is to make excuses for or cover up a problem employee's behavior. This excusing and covering up make you a co-conspirator in perpetuating the problem.

A third option is to fire a problem employee. However, statistics prove that replacing an experienced employee can cost a company as much as *double* the employee's annual salary.[10] For instance, it can cost up to $7,000 to replace a secretary who can type 80 words per minute! This cost includes advertising the position, interviewing applicants, training the new person, and getting the new secretary up to full productivity.

Perhaps the best way to remove distrust of health care professionals is to realize the cost-effectiveness of referring problem employees. Successful referral has these cost benefits:

- It retains experienced employees who already know the business, the products, the clients, and the systems.
- It increases productivity by helping a valued employee return to acceptable work performance standards.
- It decreases overhead by eliminating health costs related to personal problems, or problems associated with the use of alcohol or other drugs.
- It decreases expenses by eliminating absences and accidents caused by personal or family problems, or by the use of alcohol or other drugs.
- It is less expensive than firing the employee and bringing in a replacement.

---

[10] Specific costs available from Employee Assistance Professionals of America (EAPA), 4601 N. Fairfax Drive, Suite 1001, Arlington, VA 22203.

REVIEW

This chapter introduced you to several new terms and concepts. To check your understanding, circle T for True and F for False.

1. A manager or supervisor's personal attitudes about alcohol and other drugs may hamper referral.   T   F

2. On-the-job use of alcohol or other drugs doesn't hurt the employee's job performance.   T   F

3. Alcoholism and other drug dependence are diseases that can be treated.   T   F

4. Less than ten percent of employees refer themselves to an employee assistance program.   T   F

5. Enablers make excuses for an employee's disruptive behavior.   T   F

6. Denial and minimizing allow an employee's problem with alcohol or other drugs to continue.   T   F

7. Most managers and supervisors can effectively counsel an employee who may be using alcohol or other drugs.   T   F

8. The EAP can assist managers and supervisors in scheduling planned absences.   T   F

9. Statistics show that referral is more cost-effective than replacing a problem employee.   T   F

10. Managers and supervisors should leave diagnosing and counseling a problem employee to health care professionals.   T   F

[Key: 1. T, 2. F, 3. T, 4. F, 5. T, 6. T, 7. F, 8. T, 9. T, 10. T]

STEP FOUR
Knowing Your Resources

Now that you understand the advantages of referral, you need to know the resources available to you. If your company has an EAP, it is your primary resource for referrals. If not, other resources in the company—such as personnel, union representation, the company nurse or doctor—can be helpful. Or you might decide to refer problem employees to community resources.

If Your Company Has an Employee Assistance Program

About ten thousand private U.S. companies—including up to 80 percent of Fortune 500 companies—now have policies for the treatment and rehabilitation of employees with alcohol or other drug problems.[11] In addition, government agencies, contractors, or grantees are required by Drug-Free Workplace legislation to provide drug policies, establish a drug-free awareness program, and notify employees of what actions will be taken against drug sales and use in the workplace.

When a company has employee assistance policies, these policies are usually supported by an Employee Assistance Program (EAP), which may consist of a multi-person department or a single, EAP-certified individual. This program is implemented either inside the company or by an outside firm contracted to provide employee assistance services.

The Employee Assistance Program

The EAP may be a separate department, or it may be part of Human Resources or the Medical Department. It may be an

---

[11]Carol Cox Smith. *Recovery at Work*, San Francisco: Harper/Hazelden, 1990, p. 194.

outside firm contracted to provide EAP services. Regardless whether it operates inside or outside the company, the EAP serves many functions and assists managers and supervisors in a variety of ways.

The EAP can:
- study the company's needs and set up a system for screening and identifying problem employees.
- design a drug-free education program to comply with Drug-Free Workplace legislation.
- handle all reports needed to comply with Drug-Free Workplace legislation.
- conduct alcohol and other drug awareness and education programs for employees and management.
- evaluate/assess employees who may have a problem with alcohol or other drugs.
- advise employees who test positive in drug screening tests.
- facilitate interventions when needed.
- recommend a counseling or treatment plan for problem employees.
- counsel problem employees on an out-patient basis after they return to work.
- counsel family members when needed.
- conduct regular follow-up interviews with problem employees who are getting counseling or treatment.
- advise management on how to proceed if the employee relapses.

Perhaps the EAP's four most important functions are:
1) processing supervisory referrals
2) handling random drug testing results
3) maintaining the employee's confidentiality, and
4) training for intervention.

Processing referrals. When you refer a problem employee, the EAP will:

- assess the employee's problem or refer the employee to a selected outside health care resource for assessment.
- counsel the employee or implement the counseling or treatment plan recommended by the selected outside resource.
- inform the supervisor of any need for the employee's absence from work.
- keep in touch with the supervisor regarding the employee's situation.
- implement a follow-up plan to monitor the employee's compliance with company policies.

Because the EAP takes responsibility, your part in referral is fairly simple. When you refer a problem employee to the EAP, your responsibilities include:

1) consulting with one of the company's EAP counselors to discuss your concerns about a problem employee. At this time, the EAP will ask you to provide any documentation that will support your decision to refer the employee.
2) filling out any necessary referral forms.
3) providing copies of your documentation.
4) setting up a time for the employee to meet with the counselor.
5) notifying the problem employee of the appointed meeting time.
6) waiting for the EAP counselor to contact you with a recommendation.
7) cooperating with the EAP follow-up plan.

Random drug testing. If the problem employee tests positive in a random drug test, the EAP will take complete charge. The EAP will:

- interview the employee and assess the problem.
- review with the employee all applicable company policies.

- notify the employee of any disciplinary action.
- notify the union that disciplinary action is being taken. (The union's early involvement may encourage the problem employee to seek treatment and to follow company policies.)
- recommend a counseling or treatment plan that the employee may or may not choose to follow.
- inform the supervisor of any work-related implications.

Intervention. If you referred the employee or if an employee tests positive in a drug screening test, the EAP *may* ask you, along with others (such as co-workers, union representative, company nurse, family members) to participate in an *intervention*.

An intervention is a carefully planned conference that includes the most significant and authoritative persons in the problem employee's life. The purposes are to persuade him or her to enter a treatment program voluntarily and to detail what action the employer will take if the employee chooses not to comply.[12]

An EAP professional will teach participants how to intervene effectively and will pre-arrange the employee's admittance to a selected treatment facility. If the employee chooses not to seek treatment, the EAP will advise the employee of what disciplinary action the company will take.

Confidentiality. The Employee Assistance Program will do everything possible to protect the problem employee's privacy. EAP professionals will not tell you the results of random drug testing, nor will they inform you of the diagnosis of an employee's problem. The only information they will give you is when and for how long the employee will be absent from your department.

----

[12]Weisberg, Jeffrey and Gene Hawes. *RX for Recovery*, New York: Franklin Watts, 1989, pp. 37-38.

If the EAP counselor asks you to meet with union representatives who are concerned about the employee's rights and welfare, this meeting need not trouble you. Your confidential documentation will support your decision to refer the problem employee.

CIRCLE YES OR NO

1. Our company has an employee assistance program or department.   Yes   No
2. I am familiar with the functions of the employee assistance program in our company.   Yes   No
3. I know the EAP person to whom problem employees should be referred.   Yes   No

All three of your answers should be yes if your company provides an inside or outside employee assistance program.

If Your Company Does Not Have an EAP

If your company does not have an employee assistance program, you can refer a problem employee to other departments. Among them are:

1. Human Resources
2. Personnel
3. Medical
4. Union Issues and Representation
5. Equal Employment Opportunity
6. Other

Human Resources Department. In many companies, the EAP is part of the human resources department. If the staff includes certified addictions counselors, assessment and counseling may be done within this department. Otherwise, the department will refer the problem employee to the company's outside EAP or other resource for testing, counseling, or treatment.

Personnel Department. When a human resources department is not available, the personnel department may be your primary referral resource. This department may refer the problem employee to the appropriate department within the company or to the outside EAP or health care professional whose role it is to take referrals for that particular company.

CIRCLE YES OR NO

1. The personnel department functions as the company's employee assistance program.   Yes   No

2. Someone in the personnel department is qualified to assess a problem employee.   Yes   No

3. Someone in the personnel department can recommend an outside resource to which problem employees can be referred.   Yes   No

Your yes answers indicate that the personnel department will be a helpful resource. Your no answers mean that other departments, or an outside resource, will be more useful.

Medical Department. Because dependence on alcohol or other drugs is a disease, it may be covered by the company's health insurance plan; therefore, in some companies, EAP is part of the medical department. This arrangement assures problem employees confidentiality because their medical file is kept separate from their personnel file.

No matter what the size of your medical department— whether one nurse or a half-dozen doctors, counselors, and technicians—these health care professionals offer a wealth of information and assistance. Here are just a few examples:

- The company nurse can talk to the problem employee to get an idea of his or her general health.
- A doctor or counselor can set up a series of tests to determine the extent and nature of the employee's problem.

- More than likely, someone in this department can assess the seriousness of the problem employee's condition and recommend a treatment plan.
- The nurse, doctor, or counselor will know a community resource to which the problem employee can be referred.

CIRCLE YES OR NO

1. I am knowledgeable about the services offered by the company's medical department.   Yes   No
2. I am willing to consult the medical department if an employee assistance program is not available in our company.   Yes   No
3. Our company keeps all employees' medical files separate from personnel files.   Yes   No

A yes answer to each of these three questions indicates that the company's medical department can be a helpful resource when a problem employee needs referral.

Union Issues and Representation. Unions are deeply concerned about their members' rights and welfare. Some oppose random drug testing as an invasion of privacy; however, many unions consider the EAP a *company benefit* because it can save an employee's job. In some companies, union representatives sit on an *ad hoc* committee for alcohol and other drug issues. Or union members who themselves have been through treatment act as peer counselors.

The union wants assurance that referrals are properly handled. If a manager or supervisor documents work performance and behavior problems, maintains confidentiality, and follows company policies, the union will have no reason to object to your referring a problem employee. In fact, it may be a strong ally.

You may want to check with this department if you are unsure of the union's position regarding referral or if you want clarification of the union contract.

CAUTION: Never mention the name of an employee whom you want to refer for assessment. Confidentiality is the right of all employees, whether they belong to a union or not.

CIRCLE YES OR NO
1. There is union representation in our company. Yes No
2. I know whom to contact regarding union questions.
                                                        Yes No
3. I know that detailed, confidential documentation will answer most union objections.   Yes No

If you answered yes to question 1, you should also answer yes to 2 and 3. The union and its representatives can be powerful allies when you refer problem employees.

Equal Employment Opportunity. Your company may not have an employee assistance program, but it may have a EEO officer. Basically, the EEO officer is responsible for assuring that all employees are treated fairly in matters of hiring, promoting, and firing. Many companies carefully follow EEO practices and comply with federal government legislation to prevent discrimination in the workplace.

You might find the EEO officer especially helpful when a problem employee is a woman or minority person. Without mentioning the employee's name, you can discuss your concerns with the EEO officer and decide how to proceed so that the employee's rights are protected. As with *all* employees, your careful documentation will support your efforts to refer a minority employee.

Unless the EEO officer is a chemical dependence counselor, he or she cannot assess the employee's situation nor recommend a treatment plan. However, the officer may be able to recommend a person or department within the company or an outside program to which you can refer the problem employee. Make sure that your discussion is strictly confidential.

CIRCLE YES OR NO
1. Our organization has an EEO officer or department.
                                                    Yes   No
2. I am familiar with EEO functions.   Yes   No
3. I am knowledgeable about equal employment practices as
   they may affect a problem employee.   Yes   No

All three answers should be yes if your company has an EEO officer or department. Utilizing this resource can help prevent claims of discrimination when referring a problem employee.

Other Departments. Depending on its organizational structure, your company may have other people and programs you can tap for information and assistance. For instance, other managers or administrators, the Women's Program, or the Training Division may be helpful. Someone in these departments may have had previous experience with problem employees and be able to recommend the appropriate resource.

REMEMBER: No matter with whom you confer, you must be careful to protect the employee's confidentiality.

Legal Considerations

In some organizations, the legal department is a valuable all-around adviser. Although the legal department cannot assess or counsel a problem employee, it can and should advise managers and supervisors about the legally correct way to proceed. You may want to ask the legal department about the company's written policies concerning alcohol or other drugs, the employee's contract, any applicable union contract, or past practices that set precedents for dealing with problem employees.

In general, employees are entitled to *advance notice* of the company's policies; without advance notice, they may be entitled to a management/union hearing before you can take action. The employee's contract may prohibit you from taking certain actions, and union contracts may require that you follow *due process* before referring or disciplining a problem employee.

In addition, some state courts have set legal precedents that support the concept of "reasonable accommodation." These precedents show that some judges take a dim view of firing employees who seek treatment for alcohol or other drug problems. In these judges' view, problem employees should be given time off to seek treatment and are entitled to the same health benefits that other physically ill employees receive.

If the company does not have an EAP, the legal department may require that specific procedures be followed before you refer an employee. For instance, if the company has instituted a random drug-testing program, the legal department may prohibit you from taking separate action. Again, your detailed, confidential documentation can provide the legal basis on which you can proceed. When you *document* that an employee cannot perform the job, or that an employee's actions threaten property or the safety of others, you are following legally correct procedure.

All employees have legal rights, whether they work for a private employer or government agency, contractor, or grantee. However, while private employers may, under most circumstances, hire and fire at will, the U.S. government requires government-related employers to use constraint. For instance, the Rehabilitation Act of 1973 prohibits discrimination against drug abusers who are *able to perform their jobs*. In addition, the Comprehensive Alcohol Abuse and Alcoholism Prevention, Treatment and Rehabilitation Act of 1970 defines alcoholism as an illness and urges government-related employers to establish employee alcoholism treatment programs. Drug-Free Workplace legislation expands the responsibilities of government agencies, contractors, and grantees that contract with or receive funds from the federal government.

All U.S. citizens are entitled to Constitutional rights. You should know the basic provisions of these three Constitutional Amendments:

> 1) the Fourth Amendment gives protection against unreasonable government search and seizure without a warrant issued on the basis of probable cause;

2) the Fifth Amendment protects the employee from self-incrimination, which is giving evidence against oneself;

3) the Fourteenth Amendment provides for due process and equal protection, that is, applying the law equally to all persons.

Employees also have state civil rights that prohibit discriminatory hiring and employment practices on the basis of age, sex, race, or religion. Problem employees may claim that their constitutional or civil rights were violated or that they were harassed or suffered mental distress.

You can avoid legal battles by following these rules:

1. Always provide careful, confidential documentation.
2. Give all employees advance notice of policies concerning alcohol and other drugs.
3. Know what employment or union contracts apply and follow the due process detailed in those contracts.
4. Be aware of the employee's federal and civil rights.
5. Protect the employee's right to confidentiality.
6. Consult the EAP or legal department about the problem employee's legal rights.

CIRCLE YES OR NO

1. I am aware of every employee's legal rights.   Yes No
2. I will make sure that I am following legally correct procedures before I refer a problem employee. Yes No
3. I am careful to protect a problem employee's right to confidentiality and anonymity.   Yes No

By answering yes to each of these three questions, you are guaranteeing the problem employee's rights and protecting yourself from legal hassles.

REFERRAL RESOURCES

Complete the following list of contact persons and telephone numbers of these persons or their departments. It will provide a handy directory of resources to consult when you want to refer a problem employee.

DEPARTMENT	CONTACT PERSON	TELEPHONE
EMPLOYEE ASSISTANCE		
HUMAN RESOURCES		
PERSONNEL		
MEDICAL		
UNION		
EEO		
LEGAL		
OTHER		

COMMUNITY RESOURCES FOR REFERRAL

If your company does not provide an employee assistance program or other referral resource, you may find a community resource helpful. The following health care professionals can advise you how to proceed.

Find the names and telephone numbers of at least five of these community resources. Then you will have a directory for quick reference.

<u>RESOURCE</u>	<u>CONTACT PERSON</u>	<u>TELEPHONE</u>
HOSPITALS		
_____	_____	_____
_____	_____	_____
ALCOHOLISM TREATMENT CENTERS		
_____	_____	_____
_____	_____	_____
ALCOHOLISM COUNSELORS		
_____	_____	_____
_____	_____	_____
ALCOHOL ABUSE HOTLINE		
_____	_____	_____

DRUG TREATMENT
CENTERS

_____   _____   _____

_____   _____   _____

DRUG ABUSE
COUNSELORS

_____   _____   _____

_____   _____   _____

DRUG ABUSE
HOTLINE

_____   _____   _____

CHEMICAL DEPENDENCE
DIVISION OF COUNTY
MENTAL HEALTH CENTER

_____   _____   _____

CHEMICAL DEPENDENCE
DIVISION OF LOCAL UNIVERSITY

_____   _____   _____

DRUG DETECTING
OR TESTING SERVICES

_____   _____   _____

_____   _____   _____

NATIONAL COUNCIL ON
ALCOHOLISM AND
DRUG DEPENDENCE (NCADD)
12 WEST 21ST STREET
NEW YORK, NY 10010   _____   (212) 206-6770

Most of these resources, such as hospital treatment programs and counseling services, can assess an employee's problem and make a recommendation. After meeting with the employee and considering your written documentation, the doctor or counselor may believe that an alcohol or other drug problem exists. Depending on the severity of the problem, the professional will recommend a course of action, such as an out-patient counseling program or in-patient treatment.

Sometimes the problem is not related to alcohol or other drugs. Work performance may be affected by a marital, family, or financial problem, or by job-related stress. In that case, the professional might refer the employee to another resource, such as a marriage counselor, family support group, or stress-management program. With a professional diagnosis, you know when alcohol or drugs are the culprits—and when they are not.

The two lists you compiled in this chapter give you a useful directory of resources either from whom you can get information or to whom you can refer a problem employee. *As long as you do not mention the employee's name,* you can freely discuss the situation with anyone inside or outside the organization. However, talking about a problem employee does not help that employee, nor does it relieve the department of the turmoil he or she creates. Only *referral* starts a problem-resolution process that benefits everyone.

REVIEW

This is a multiple-choice quiz of terms and concepts you learned in this chapter. Circle the letter of the correct answer.

1. Outside referral resources include:
    a. counseling professionals
    b. a hospital
    c. treatment centers for alcohol and other drug dependence
    d. all of the above

2. If an employee's drop in work performance seems to be related to financial problems, the manager or supervisor can refer the employee to:
    a. the company's EAP
    b. a community financial resource
    c. a chemical dependence professional
    d. both a. and b. above

3. Government agencies, contractors, and grantees are constrained by:
    a. Constitutional rights
    b. state civil rights
    c. Drug-Free Workplace legislation
    d. all of the above

4. An in-company Employee Assistance Program is effective when:
    a. management fully supports the department's functions
    b. more than 25 percent of the company tests positive for drugs
    c. managers and supervisors handle problem employees themselves
    d. no one in the organization knows about it

5. One of an employee's legal rights is:
    a. the right to representation by a union
    b. the right to paid vacations
    c. the right to advance notice of alcohol and other drug policies
    d. the right to refuse random drug testing without consequences

6. A supervisor's best defense against legal hassles is:
    a. never getting involved in referring a problem employee
    b. detailed, confidential documentation
    c. informing his or her supervisor of what employee is involved
    d. giving the problem employee a second chance

7. An employee who is caught using alcohol on the job should be:
    a. fired on the spot
    b. helped by a co-worker
    c. given "reasonable accommodation," which is the opportunity to seek alcoholism treatment voluntarily
    d. given two weeks' notice

8. The inside or outside EAP can perform the following function:
    a. arranging for assessment of the employee's problem
    b. giving the problem employee a stern lecture
    c. alerting other departments that an employee has an alcohol or other drug problem
    d. making sure an employee's personnel file includes all EAP reports

9. An outside employee assistance company:
    a. works on a contract basis
    b. performs the same functions as an inside Employee Assistance Department
    c. offers on-site or off-site services
    d. all of the above

10. If a company does not have an employee assistance department, managers and supervisors can:
    a. ignore problem employees
    b. counsel problem employees themselves
    c. consult their directory of in-company and outside-company resources
    d. wait at least one month to see if the problem employee straightens out

[ANSWERS: 1. d, 2. d, 3. d, 4. a, 5. c, 6. b, 7. c, 8. a, 9. d, 10. c.]

STEP FIVE
Taking Action

Let's assume that you are concerned about a problem employee and have completed these four steps in referral:

1. Documenting work performance problems
2. Identifying the problem employee
3. Eliminating enabling—the principal barrier to referral
4. Knowing your resources

Now what? Now you take action. You *confront the problem employee* and *detail how you expect the employee to improve performance.*

Confrontation has four goals:

1. To let the problem employee know what you have observed.
2. To give the problem employee a chance to respond.
3. To detail what you, the supervisor, expect the employee to do to achieve satisfactory performance.
4. To explain what will happen if performance does not improve.

OBSTACLES TO CONFRONTATION

Many supervisors dislike confronting a problem employee. Here are some of their reasons. Check any reasons that you think apply to you.

____ I feel intimidated when an employee gets angry.

____ I allow the employee to convince me I'm wrong.

____ It's the employee's word against mine.

____ I don't want to make a moral judgment.

____ I feel uncomfortable confronting employees of the opposite sex.

____ I find it difficult to criticize other people.
____ I feel incompetent to deal with an employee's excuses.
____ I don't believe the confrontation will do any good.
____ I don't think others in the company will support my actions.
____ I am worried that my actions may bring trouble from other
      employees or other departments.
____ Other (explain)

_____

_____

Whatever your reasons for avoiding confrontation, those reasons are preventing a problem employee from getting help. They are also preventing you from being as effective a manager or supervisor as you can be.

To remove these obstacles, you need to take three steps:
1) Confront your own feelings.
2) Practice confrontation with a safe, trusted friend or business associate.
3) Plan for a successful confrontation.

Confront your own feelings. The reasons you checked above may reveal your own feelings of fear or inadequacy. Perhaps you are afraid that you cannot deal effectively with serious problems in your department. Perhaps you have tried and failed to help problem employees in the past, and now you feel inadequate to handle these complex relationships. If you confront your own feelings, you may discover that they keep you from being an effective manager or supervisor.

Employees have a right to be supervised. They have a right to know what you want them to do. They have a right to take corrective action that will preserve their job status. Your silence is the same as your approval.

If you want to be effective, you must *learn to confront problem employees.* Taking the steps explained below will help you deal successfully with problem employees and improve overall performance in your department.

Practice confrontation with a safe, trusted friend or business associate. Practice helps you feel more confident when you confront a problem employee. To practice confrontation, ask one of the company's EAP professionals to play the part of an employee while you enact what you plan to say and do. Or ask another manager or supervisor, or a friend or business associate, to pretend to be the employee.

During these rehearsals, you can prepare how you will respond to the employee's embarrassment, anger, or excuses. After a few practice sessions, you will be prepared to deal with the employee's reactions.

Plan for a successful confrontation. There are three skills needed for a successful confrontation:

- Stating the problem objectively.
- Listening to the employee's responses.
- Giving the employee clear options.

Skill 1: Stating the problem objectively

- Make sure your statements refer to the incidents you have documented—not to your personal opinions or conclusions.
- Try not to be judgmental, critical, or authoritarian. Rather, establish a forum for discussion by asking for the employee's solutions to these problems.
- Realize that work-related problems, such as poor equipment or insufficient staffing, may be causing the problem. Be willing to work with the employee to find a problem-solving solution.

Here are examples of ways to discuss performance problems. Practice these or similar statements before you meet with a problem employee.

Confronting Problem Employees

To establish a problem-solving atmosphere, avoid statements that judge, threaten, or accuse. *Never* accuse the employee of having a problem with alcohol or other drugs.

JUDGMENTAL	NONJUDGMENTAL
"You obviously don't care about your job, or you wouldn't be absent so often."	"I have documented six absences this month. This is excessive absence and could cost you your job. Can you explain these absences?"
"I'm tired of having to deal with all the problems you cause."	"I have received three complaints that you are picking arguments with other employees. What do you plan to do to improve your work relationships?"
"The way you've been acting, I feel sure you have a problem with alcohol or other drugs."	"In the past three months, you've had three accidents on the job. Your attitude has changed. What do you think is causing these problems?"

Skill 2: Listening to the employee's response

- Give the employee time to respond. Do not interrupt.
- Sit back and assume an attitude of concerned attention.
- Expect a chemically dependent employee to make excuses and try to talk you out of taking a firm stand.
- Show respect for the employee's ideas and feelings. Acknowledge the employee's responses in a positive way: "I see what you mean" or "You have a good point."
- Repeat (paraphrase) what the employee says to make sure you understand the response: "So you think your absences are caused by family problems?" or "Are you saying that those accidents were coincidental?"
- Try to get the employee to talk openly. Instead of saying "I think . . ." ask, "What do *you* think?"

Skill 3: Giving the employee clear options

When you believe the employee has had sufficient time to answer your questions, tell the employee what you expect. Repeat your statement that this drop in work performance is not acceptable and give the employee a *dated warning*, like this:

> "Your attendance must meet departmental standards by the end of this month, or I will take further action."

or

> "If there are any more complaints about your attitude from other employees, I will refer this matter to our EAP."

or

> "I don't believe there is a work-related reason why your performance has declined. I am concerned that a personal or health reason may be causing the problem. I must insist that you consult with our medical department before you return to work."

or

> "If you come to work in that condition again, I will personally take you to EAP for evaluation."

or

> "We have talked about this problem twice before. Still you continue to have these problems at work. Because I care about you, I have set up an appointment with Miss Gonzalez in EAP. I want you to talk to her before you come back to work."

These statements give the employee a clear message: "I expect you to straighten out your work performance problem or I will take further action."

This clear-cut message says that the employee must take responsibility for improving work performance and that you will no longer tolerate excuses. It also conveys the message that *you care* about the employee and the employee's status with the company.

Skill 4: Planning for a successful confrontation

Planning is essential for a successful confrontation. Use the following checklist to make sure you are prepared to discuss a work performance problem.

CONFRONTATION CHECKLIST

Before a confrontation

____ 1. Notify the employee of the time and place of your meeting.
____ 2. Notify the employee of the purpose of the meeting.
____ 3. Prepare for the meeting by reviewing company policy regarding problem employees.
____ 4. Also review the employee's past performance for comparison with present performance.
____ 5. Make sure you know the performance standards for the employee's job.
____ 6. Consult EAP if you plan to refer the employee.
____ 7. Make sure you and the employee can talk privately for a comfortable block of time.
____ 8. Review your documentation.
____ 9. Practice what you will say and do.
____ 10. Protect the employee's privacy. Do not discuss work performance with anyone except the EAP professional or other person to whom you plan to refer the employee for assessment.

During the confrontation

____ 11. Stick to the topic of work performance. Do not be drawn into an argument about personalities, age, race, religion, or sex.
____ 12. Review with the employee the purpose of the meeting.
____ 13. Review with the employee the incidents you have documented.
____ 14. Clarify work performance standards.
____ 15. Ask for the employee's response.
____ 16. Encourage the employee to suggest ways to improve work performance.
____ 17. Offer to support the employee's plans for improvement.
____ 18. State the employee's options clearly.

_____ 19. Set a time to review any improvements in the employee's performance.
_____ 20. Summarize the meeting so that both you and the employee know what was agreed upon, who is to do what, and when performance will be reviewed.

After the confrontation
_____ 21. Write a follow-up memorandum covering the main points and place it in a confidential file. Add any comments or corrections the employee makes.
_____ 22. Continue to document any further problems.
_____ 23. Take *immediate* action if the employee fails to improve. For instance, if the employee comes to work in such a condition that he or she cannot work, immediately escort the employee to the Employee Assistance Department.
_____ 24. Note on your calendar to check the employee's work performance on a specified date.
_____ 25. Review the discussion for ways in which you can improve your confrontation skills.

Realize that your confrontation may cause a chemically dependent employee to quit the job before you can complete the referral. Or the employee may beg for another chance or put on a show of bravado. Hopefully the employee will realize that there is a problem and that it is time to get help. Anything can happen, from hostility to tears, but you should not be swayed. Your concerned, caring—yet firm—confrontation is the best possible thing you can do to help a problem employee.

What if the employee balks at the confrontation and refuses referral? Then the supervisor must make an ultimatum, like this:

"Either you meet with an employee assistance counselor, or I will have no choice but (to let you go) (to take disciplinary action)."

Hopefully, the supervisor's "either/or" stance will force the problem employee to believe that referral is the better option.

PUT YOUR CONFRONTATION SKILLS TO THE TEST

Case 1: Harry and the Driver. Shipping supervisor Harry Morton learns that the teenage son of one of his best drivers was arrested last week for robbery. Later Harry observes that the same driver is falling behind on deliveries. Checking further, Harry discovers that the driver has been involved in two minor accidents in the past week. Harry fears that the driver's family troubles are causing these work-related problems; however, he realizes that other reasons, such as health or financial problems, may be distracting the driver from his usual top-notch performance.

Harry documents these facts and decides to confront the driver. He asks the driver to meet with him privately and tells the driver that he wants to discuss work performance. During the meeting, Harry reviews the facts and asks for an explanation. Harry assures the driver that he is a valued employee and that the company can help him work out any personal problems that are affecting his performance.

The driver becomes belligerent, loudly claiming that he is doing as good a job as anyone else. Harry calmly states that the driver's performance is below standards and must show improvement by the end of the month. Harry adds: "The next time you fail to make a scheduled delivery or have an accident, I will take further action." Two days later, the driver is arrested for speeding.

1. What do you think of the way Harry handled the situation?

---

2. What should Harry do now?

_____

_____

_____

Check your answers with the answers given below.

Answer 1. Harry handled the situation well. He acted quickly to avoid letting things get worse. He had sufficient documentation to confront the driver, and he did so in a caring yet firm way. He invited the driver to help solve the problem. He met the driver's anger with a firm statement of options.

Answer 2. Harry should document the speeding incident and take further action. He should suggest that the employee self-refer. If the employee refuses, Harry should discuss the situation with EAP and arrange an appointment for the employee to be evaluated. Harry should tell the driver that no further deliveries can be made without the assurance of safety.

Case 2: A Banking Error. Charlotte Teghorn, a banking vice president, began to receive complaints about a newly promoted teller supervisor. The supervisor, Martha McAllister, was rude to tellers, made numerous errors, and sometimes smelled of bourbon during working hours. Charlotte thought that Martha was simply feeling the pressure of her new promotion; nonetheless, Charlotte began to document these incidents.

On the chance that some complaints were motivated by other tellers' jealousy of Martha's promotion, Charlotte made a point of observing and documenting Martha's work performance herself. After a few days, Martha had documented ten separate incidents of below-standard work performance.

Charlotte decided to take action. She asked Martha to meet with her to discuss work performance problems. During the meeting, Charlotte reviewed the list of complaints and errors. She asked Martha to suggest ways to improve her performance and assured her that she would support Martha's efforts to change.

Martha seemed unaware that her performance was below standards and immediately apologized. She claimed that she felt insecure about her new job. She asked Martha to give her time to get used to her new responsibilities. Charlotte suggested a week of additional training, which Martha gladly accepted. Charlotte set a follow-up date for two weeks following the training period.

Instead of improving, Martha's performance deteriorated further. After Charlotte documented several new incidents, she talked to the company's outside EAP and sent copies of her documentation. Following a telephone conference, the EAP agreed that referral was indicated. Charlotte made an appointment for Martha to see the EAP the following afternoon.

When Charlotte told Martha about the appointment, Martha protested that she could handle her own problems and that she thought Charlotte was overreacting. Charlotte firmly told Martha that she would not accept any further excuses and that she was taking action. Martha could either keep the appointment with the EAP or lose her job. Martha agreed to keep the appointment.

1. What do you think of the way Charlotte handled this situation?

_____

_____

_____

2. What should Charlotte do now?

_____

_____

_____

Check your answers with the answers below.

Answer 1. Charlotte handled this situation in a caring, competent, professional manner. She had ample documentation to support the belief that Martha had a problem with alcohol or other drugs; yet she did not accuse, blame, or diagnose. Instead, she provided additional training to improve Martha's confidence, at the same time setting a timetable to meet standards. When problems continued, Charlotte followed company policy and referred Martha to EAP.

Answer 2. Charlotte should continue to document any further incidents, protecting Martha's privacy. She should cooperate with, and participate in, if asked, any intervention planned by EAP and in any counseling or treatment plan.

SUPERVISOR'S REFERRAL CHECKLIST

Complete this checklist to make sure you have followed each of the five steps of referral. Include this list in the problem employee's confidential file.

Employee's Code_____

Department_____

1. Documenting work performance problems.
    ____ I completed written records of work performance problems that include date, place, what happened, and who was involved.
    ____ I avoided diagnosing the employee's problem.
    ____ I kept all records confidential.
    ____ I did not discuss the employee's performance with other supervisors, employees, or customers.

2. Identifying problem employees.
    ____ I identified a work-related problem in my department.
    ____ I examined the impact of this problem on my department's productivity.
    ____ I reviewed work performance standards for this employee's job.
    ____ I observed changes in the employee's behavior.
    ____ I noticed signs of family dysfunction.
    ____ I analyzed complaints received from co-workers and others.

3.   Eliminating enabling—the principal barrier to referral.
   ____ I did not let my attitudes about alcohol and other drugs interfere with prompt handling of this problem.
   ____ I did not let my personal use of alcohol or other drugs enable the employee to continue causing work-related problems.
   ____ I did not deny or minimize the impact of the problem employee's behavior on departmental productivity.
   ____ I admitted that I personally am not qualified to counsel this employee.
   ____ I realized that my careful documentation was my best defense against legal, union, EEO or other repercussions.
   ____ I made plans to cover this employee's absence from work.

4.   Knowing your resources.
   ____ I reviewed company policies regarding referring problem employees.
   ____ I contacted the company's EAP or other authorized department and discussed my documentation before confronting the problem employee.
   ____ I provided the EAP with copies of my documentation.
   ____ I conscientiously protected the employee's privacy and legal rights.
   ____ I notified the employee's union that I am making a referral to the EAP.

5.   Taking action.
   ____ I examined my personal feelings about confronting this employee.
   ____ I practiced the confrontation with another supervisor or trusted associate.
   ____ I used the four skills of successful confrontation.
   ____ I clearly stated what I expected the employee to do and set a timetable for improved performance.
   ____ I will continue to document further incidents involving this employee.

Conclusion

When you use the five steps of referral, you will begin to see positive differences in your department. First, problem employees may decide to seek professional help or to enter treatment. This change will give you more time and energy to focus on other departmental matters. It will also improve employee morale, efficiency, and productivity. In a few months, you will see the overall costs of mistakes, absenteeism, downtime, accidents, and health claims decrease.

Second, you will see positive differences even if problem employees decide *not* to seek help. In this case, by your following the five steps of referral, the employee clearly knows the consequences of continued use of alcohol or other drugs. When you enforce those consequences, you nudge the chemically dependent person closer to seeking help. In addition, your action shows other employees that you are committed to maintaining a drug-free workplace. This firm stance reflects well on your managerial or supervisory ability—an impression that can make a difference in your career.

Referral is the most effective way to deal with problem employees. Even if you feel uncomfortable with the process at first, you will gain confidence as you see positive results in your department. Making this process an integral part of your managerial style is the best way to ensure a safe, healthy, productive workplace for everyone.

MEETING YOUR OBJECTIVES

Looking back to page xi of this book, rate how well you accomplished your objectives. Check the line that best describes your achievements.

		Yes	No	Sometimes
1.	I can recognize problem employees in my department.	___	___	_____
2.	I expect to see an increase in productivity.	___	___	_____
3.	I understand that referring problem employees will decrease health costs.	___	___	_____
4.	I perceive an improvement in departmental morale since referring a problem employee.	___	___	_____
5.	I know how to refer problem employees to the company EAP or other resource.	___	___	_____
6.	I know that careful documentation will protect me from legal, union, or EEO complaints.	___	___	_____
7.	I can recognize when I enable a problem employee.	___	___	_____
8.	I am able to focus my time, energy, and talent on my job, rather than on dealing with a problem employee.	___	___	_____

SUPERVISOR'S REFERRAL CONTRACT

Here is one way to encourage yourself to *use* what you have learned: Sign a contract with yourself. This action underscores the importance of referral and motivates you to make referral an integral part of your departmental operations.

Keep this informal contract where you can refer to it easily. Use it as a quick reminder of the key role you play in turning problem employees into successes.

I, _____, agree to refer all problem employees to the company's EAP or other appropriate resource. I will:

1. Follow the five steps of referral.

2. Document below-standard work performance.

3. Write generic or specific work performance standards for each job description.

4. Examine my own attitudes about referring problem employees.

5. Take advantage of the company's EAP.

6. Improve my confrontational skills.

Signature _____

Date _____

For Further Reading:

Books

Bissell, LeClair, and Haberman, Paul W. *Alcoholism in the Professions*. New York: Oxford University Press, Inc., 1984.

Cox Smith, Carol. *Recovery at Work: A Clean and Sober Career Guide*. San Francisco: Harper & Row/Hazelden, 1990.

Crosby, Linda, and Bissell, LeClair. *To Care Enough: Intervention with Impaired Professionals*. Minneapolis: Johnson Institute, 1989.

Fleming, Martin. *Commitment to Sobriety: A Relapse Guide for Adults in Recovery*. Minneapolis: Johnson Institute, 1991.

Googins, Bradley K. *Work/Family Conflicts: Private Lives—Public Responses*. New York: Auburn House, 1991.

Johnson, Vernon. *Intervention: How to Help Someone Who Doesn't Want Help*. Minneapolis: Johnson Institute, 1986.

Booklets

Blair, Brenda R. *Supervisors and Managers as Enablers*, 1987. Also available in Spanish.

Blair, Brenda R. *The Supervisor's Role in Early Recovery*, 1991.

Crosby, Linda and Bissell, LeClair. *Enabling in the Health Professions*, 1991.

Enabling in the Workplace, 1991.

For more information or to order any of these publications, call toll-free:

Johnson Institute
1-800-231-5165
In Canada, call: 1-800-447-6660
In Minnesota, call: 1-800-247-0484 or 612-831-1630